Montana
on my mind

Photography by Michael S. Sample and Larry Mayer

First Banks
Montana Region
Members First Bank System

FALCON PRESS

acknowledgments

The authors gratefully acknowledge permission to reprint the following material:

Page 4 from "My Country" by Arapooish, Chief of the Crows, *Contributions to the Historical Society of Montana,* Vol. IX. Courtesy of the Montana Historical Society.

Pages 18 and 53 from *Montana: High, Wide, and Handsome* by Joseph Kinsey Howard. Copyright © 1943, 1959 by Yale University Press. Excerpt on page 18 by Donald Culross Peattie.

Page 24 from *The Last Hero: A Biography of Gary Cooper* by Larry Swindell. Copyright © 1980 by Larry Swindell. Reprinted by permission of Doubleday and Company, Inc.

Page 28 from *Beef, Leather and Grass* by Edmund Randolph. Copyright © 1981 by the University of Oklahoma Press.

Page 30 from *The Journals of Lewis and Clark* by Bernard DeVoto. Copyright 1953 by Bernard DeVoto. Copyright © renewed 1981 by Avis DeVoto. Reprinted by permission of Houghton Mifflin Company.

Page 40 from *The Generous Years: Remembrances of a Frontier Boyhood* by Chet Huntley. Copyright © 1968 by Chet Huntley. Reprinted by permission of Random House, Inc.

Page 44 from *Bury my Heart at Wounded Knee: An Indian History of the American West* by Dee Brown. Copyright © 1970 by Dee Brown. Reprinted by permission of Henry Holt and Company, Inc.

Page 50 from *The Pass* by Thomas Savage. Reprinted by permission of Doubleday and Company, Inc.

Pages 58 and 72 from *A River Runs through It* by Norman Maclean. © 1976 by The University of Chicago.

Page 60 from *A Day Late and a Dollar Short* by Spike Van Cleve. The Lowell Press, Kansas City, Mo., 1981.

Pages 62 and 95 from *Montana: Images of the Past* by William E. Farr and K. Ross Toole. Pruett Publishing Co., Boulder, Colo., 1978.

Page 64, "The Yellowstone" by Wallace D. McRae, September 1986. Reprinted by permission of the author.

Pages 66, 69, and 78 from *Montana Wilderness* by Steve Woodruff and Don Schwennesen, photographs by Carl Davaz, 1984, The Missoulian and The Lowell Press, Kansas City, Mo.

Page 70 from *Grass Roots* by Stan Lynde. Copyright © 1984, 1985 by Stan Lynde and Grass Roots Publishers.

Page 80 from *The Hunter's Guide to Montana* by Mark Henckel. Copyright © 1985 by Falcon Press Publishing Co., Inc.

Page 86 from *Anatomy of a Fisherman* by Robert Traver. Reprinted by permission of the author.

Page 89 reprinted from *Pioneering in Montana* by Granville Stuart, published by the University of Nebraska Press.

Page 92 from *Montana: Our Land and People* by William Lang and Rex Myers. Pruett Publishing Co., Boulder, Colo., 1979.

Page 96 from *Montana: An Uncommon Land* by K. Ross Toole. Copyright © 1959 by the University of Oklahoma Press.

Page 112 from *Tenting on the Plains: General Custer in Kansas and Texas* by Elizabeth Bacon Custer, with an Introduction by Jane R. Stewart. New edition copyright 1971 by the University of Oklahoma Press.

Page 114 from *The Big Sky* by A.B. Guthrie. Copyright 1950 by A.B. Guthrie, Jr. Copyright © renewed 1977 by A.B. Guthrie, Jr. Reprinted by permission of Houghton Mifflin Company.

Credits

Publishers: Michael S. Sample and Bill Schneider of Falcon Press,

Cover design: Linda McCray

Cover art: Gwynn Mundinger

Photo editors: Bill Schneider, Jeri Walton

Layout: Bill Schneider

Editor: Marnie Hagmann

Typesetting: DD Dowden, Barbara Stewart

Front cover photos: Michael S. Sample (Lake Fork of Rock Creek near Red Lodge), Tom Warren, Department of Fish, Wildlife and Parks (bitterroot)

Back cover photos: Larry Mayer (hang glider), Michael S. Sample (grizzly, marsh marigolds, horses)

Inside photos: Michael S. Sample (MSS), Larry Mayer (LM)

All prepress work by Falcon Press, Helena, Montana

Printed in Japan

For extra copies of this book

Write to Falcon Press, P.O. Box 279, Billings, MT 59103 or call toll-free 1-800-592-BOOK (in Montana) or 1-800-582-BOOK (outside Montana).

introduction

"Montana On My Mind" is a collection of outstanding photographs of one of America's most scenic and least known states. It is a photobiography of a state deeply loved by two of its talented citizens—Michael Sample and Larry Mayer. It is interlaced with rich quotations by famous folk who know this land and its people well. The First Banks of Montana are pleased to make this excellent publication available in conjunction with the 1989 Montana Centennial celebration.

First Bank System in Montana is comprised of eleven banks, one trust company with five offices, and one insurance company with three offices. It has a long history of financial commitment to the state's economic growth. Several of the state's First Banks opened their doors to customers more than a century ago when Montana was still only a territory.

Our strong financial commitment to Montana continues—but there is more. And that is the personal commitment of our employees—Montanans all—to enhance the state in which they have chosen to live and work. Community involvement and civic pride have been a part of their lives in Montana, since its pioneer days—and this commitment will continue to grow with each succeeding year.

Our banking system has always sought to be the foremost financial services organization in Montana. To maintain this goal, we are guided by four basic beliefs:

Customers will determine the ultimate fate of our organization. Creating excellent value for customers is the key to our success. Employees as individuals are our most valuable resource and as a team our source of competitive advantage. Communities in which we conduct business are better off for our presence. We work as partners with our communities, making them healthy and prosperous places to live and work. Shareholders have a right to expect a superior return on their investment in our company.

First Banks have been a part of Montana long before its Centennial Year...we expect to be a part of the Montana scene for many years, well beyond 1989.

We hope you enjoy "Montana On My Mind" as much as the First Banks of Montana enjoy bringing it to you.

William Strausburg
Managing Director
Montana Region, First Bank System
March 15, 1988

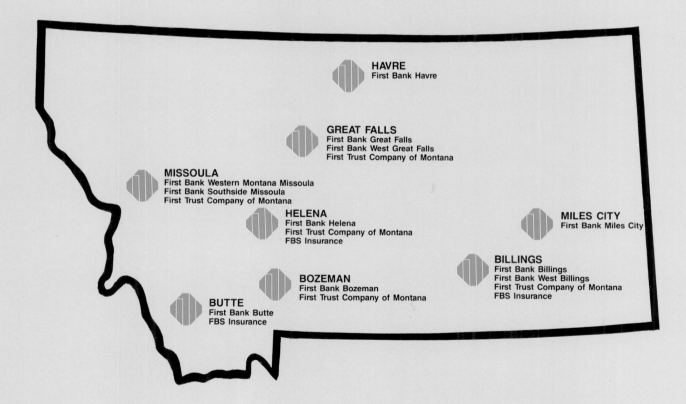

HAVRE
First Bank Havre

GREAT FALLS
First Bank Great Falls
First Bank West Great Falls
First Trust Company of Montana

MISSOULA
First Bank Western Montana Missoula
First Bank Southside Missoula
First Trust Company of Montana

HELENA
First Bank Helena
First Trust Company of Montana
FBS Insurance

MILES CITY
First Bank Miles City

BILLINGS
First Bank Billings
First Bank West Billings
First Trust Company of Montana
FBS Insurance

BOZEMAN
First Bank Bozeman
First Trust Company of Montana

BUTTE
First Bank Butte
FBS Insurance

> " *The Crow country . . . is a good country. The Great Spirit has put it exactly in the right place; while you are in it you fare well; whenever you go out of it, whichever way you travel you fare worse. If you go to the south, you have to wander over great barren plains; the water is warm and bad and you meet with fever and ague. To the north it is cold; the winters are long and bitter and there is no grass; you can not keep horses there but must travel with dogs. What is a country without horses? . . . To the east they dwell in villages; they live well, but they drink the muddy waters of the Missouri—that is bad. A Crow's dog would not drink such water. . . . The Crow country is exactly in the right place. It has snowy mountains and sunny plains, all kinds of climates and good things for every season. When the summer heats scorch the prairies, you can draw up under the mountains, where the air is sweet and cool, the grass fresh, and the bright streams come tumbling out of the snow banks. There you can hunt the elk, the deer and the antelope when their skins are fit for dressing; there you will find plenty of white bears and mountain sheep.*
>
> "*In the autumn when your horses are fat and strong from the mountain pastures you can go down into the plains and hunt the buffalo, or trap beaver on the streams. And when winter comes on, you can take shelter in the woody bottoms along the rivers.* "

Arapooish, a Crow chief,
Contributions to the
Historical Society of Montana, Vol. IX

A bull elk, antlers still in velvet, enjoying a lush spring meadow   MSS

Glacial tarn on the Continental Divide in Glacier National Park   MSS

At the Crow Fair,
Crow Agency   LM

Palisade Falls in the Gallatin Range south of Bozeman MSS

Horses graze along the Little Bighorn River near the Custer Battlefield   MSS

Spawning brown trout in the Gardner River in the Montana portion of Yellowstone National Park   MSS

Bison cow and half-hour-old calf   MSS

Clouds streaming over the Garden Wall in Glacier National Park   MSS

Early emerging marsh marigolds partially encased in frozen spring runoff   MSS

Sunset over Noxon Rapids Reservoir near Thompson Falls MSS

Nanny and two kids grazing with the
scenic backdrop of Reynolds Peak
in Glacier National Park MSS

Native cutthroat MSS

The Yellowstone River and Paradise Valley south of Livingston LM

Bull moose at sunrise   MSS

Native grassland on Crown Butte near Augusta   LM

Bull River and Cabinet Mountains near Troy   MSS

East Front of the Bridger Mountains near Bozeman   MSS

Echo Peak and Expedition Lake in the Hilgard Basin of the southern Madison Range   MSS

Prinz Ridge in the Bitterroot Mountains   MSS

The Pioneer and Tobacco Root mountains LM

“ *The western skyline before us was filled high with a steel-blue army of mountains, drawn in battalions of peaks and reefs and gorges and crags as far along the entire rim of the earth as could be seen.* ”

Ivan Doig,
This House of Sky

The Bitterroot Mountains MSS

Last look of the day at the Absaroka Mountains MSS

" *Colorado is high, having more peaks within its borders than any other state. Wyoming is wide, with the breadth of the plains between the Big Horns and the Grand Tetons. California is handsome, with a splendor of success. It takes all three adjectives to describe Montana.* **"**

Donald Culross Peattie,
Montana: High, Wide, and Handsome

The Chinese Wall in the Bob Marshall Wilderness   LM

The Big Hole Valley south of Jackson   MSS

Bighorn Canyon National Recreation Area   LM

Light dancing on Whitefish Lake near Whitefish   MSS

Sunset at Makoshika State Park near Glendive   MSS

Hunter's moon over a windmill south of Roundup   LM

Fort Peck Reservoir from above   LM

Thunder Mountain and Lake Fork of Rock Creek in the Beartooth Mountains near Red Lodge   MSS

Swallowtail butterfly and Indian paintbrush   MSS

Red squirrel   MSS

Mountain cottontail and lupine   MSS

Whitetail fawn   MSS

Meadowlark, Montana's state bird   LM

Mule deer doe and buck MSS

Water ouzel, or dipper MSS

Band of bighorn rams MSS

Long-tailed weasel, or ermine, with winter coat MSS

Young great horned owl MSS

Elephanthead flowers along Lost Trail Creek in the West Big Hole MSS

> *Beyond the river the landscape was pretty much as God had made it, and when one's eye reached up into the mountains, he saw exactly what Lewis and Clark had seen. Moreover, he breathed the same clean, crisp air from which the pioneers had drawn much of their strength. . . . Above and around all there was an incredible, restful, yet somehow vital stillness, punctuated by the meadowlarks.*
>
> Edmund Randolph,
> Beef, Leather and Grass

Warren Peak in the Anaconda-Pintler Wilderness west of Butte MSS

Crevasse in Sperry Glacier in Glacier National Park   MSS

Bison and elk along the Gardner River   MSS

Pronghorns on the National Bison Range near Moiese   MSS

“ *Thursday April 25th 1805 . . . . I had a most pleasing view of the country, particularly of the wide and fertile vallies formed by the missouri and the yellowstone rivers . . . . the whol face of the country was covered with herds of Buffaloe, Elk & Antelopes; deer are also abundant, but keep themselves more concealed in the woodland.* ”

Meriwether Lewis,
The Journals of Lewis and Clark

Elk on original prairie habitat north of Hardin   MSS

Bison crossing Mission Creek on the National Bison Range near Moiese   MSS

Wild Horse Island, largest in Flathead Lake, with the Mission Mountains on the horizon   LM

Flathead River near West Glacier   MSS

> ❝ *The plain that commands a view of the lake is one of the most fertile in the mountainous regions. The Flat Head river runs through it and extends more than 200 miles to the North East. It is wide and deep, abounding with fish and lined with wood.* ❞

Pierre-Jean deSmet,
Letters and Sketches with
Narratives of a Year's Residence
Among the Indians

Large rainbow trout feeding at Giant Springs Heritage State Park in Great Falls   MSS

Fishing on Upper Quartz Lake in the North Fork of the Flathead Drainage   MSS

Cattle feeding after a new snow near Lewistown   LM

Starting young on a rodeo bull   LM

Vestige of a homesteader's struggle in the Pryor Mountains south of Billings   MSS

" *For most women the only real reason for going west was to found a new home, and the dream of many an emigrating female was a snug log cabin nestling in some pleasant valley. Log cabins were traditional abodes of pioneers from the time of the first eastern settlements, and their construction had become a national craft. A skilled artisan could put one together with only an ax and an augur, using no nails or other pieces of metal. He sealed his logs together with wooden pins, chinked the cracks with mud, swung the doors on leather hinges, and fastened them with wood latches.* "

Dee Brown,
The Gentle Tamers

Middle Smith River south of Great Falls MSS

> *Before me I saw a plain unbroken by ravines, gently descending, for a distance of two miles, to the broad Missouri with its low, grassy banks, while beyond, I beheld the Smith River as it runs through the beautiful valley and unites its waters with those of the great Missouri. This scenery, composed of valleys and rivers, flanked by smoothly rounded table lands, formed a picture never to be forgotten.*

Paris Gibson,
"The Founding of Great Falls"

White cliffs of the Missouri near Fort Benton   MSS

Along the West Rosebud River near Columbus   MSS

The Bozeman Trail and the Crazy Mountains near Livingston MSS

" . . . *Montana is a* last Frontier; *there is no more ultimate West.* **"**

Leslie Fiedler,
Montana; or the End of Jean-Jacques Rousseau

Beaver lodge on Beaver Creek in the Madison Range MSS

Aging cabin east of Helena in the Big Belt Mountains   MSS

Seedlings encased in ice near a rushing mountain stream   MSS

Small spring tributary to the Jocko River near St. Ignatius   MSS

Summer growth along Clark Fork River near Paradise   MSS

Indian paintbrush covering a hillside near Hyalite Lake in the Gallatin Range south of Bozeman MSS

Prairie smoke MSS

Sugarbowl MSS

Pasque flower MSS

Rock Creek east of Missoula MSS

Our land is more valuable than your money. It will last forever. It will not even perish by the flames of fire. As long as the sun shines and the waters flow, this land will be here to give life to men and animals. We cannot sell the lives of men and animals; therefore we cannot sell this land. It was put here for us by the Great Spirit and we cannot sell it because it does not belong to us. You can count your money and burn it within the nod of a buffalo's head, but only the Great Spirit can count the grains of sand and the blades of grass of these plains. As a present to you, we will give you anything we have that you can take with you; but the land, never.

A Blackfoot chief,
Bury my Heart at Wounded Knee

Unnamed waterfall on Gunsight Mountain in Glacier National Park   MSS

Bowman Valley in Glacier National Park   MSS

Mount Gould near Many Glacier in Glacier National Park   MSS

Fluted rock along McDonald Creek in Glacier National Park   MSS

Mountain goats at last light   MSS

Tepees   LM

Evening primrose   MSS

"*In my life until then I had never seen the sidehills come so green, the coulees stay so spongy with runoff. A right amount of wet evidently could sweeten the universe.* "

Ivan Doig,
English Creek

Cow moose and calf in late spring snowfall   MSS

Lush hillside near Jewel Basin   MSS

Bison filing through drifted snow   MSS

" . . . the snow fell softly from a gauze sky, great lazy flakes drifting down . . . . The mildness after the blizzard hung like a curtain about them . . . "

Thomas Savage,
The Pass

Skiers on a winter trek   MSS

Horses wait out the storm MSS

> **"** *It seemed like Mother Nature was sure agreeable that day when the little black colt came to the range world, and tried to get a footing with his long wobblety legs on the brown prairie sod. Short stems of new green grass was trying to make their way up thru the last year's faded growth, and reaching for the sun's warm rays. Taking in all that could be seen, felt, and inhaled, there was no day, time, nor place that could beat that spring morning on the sunny side of the low prairie butte where Smoky the colt was foaled.* **"**

Will James,
Smoky

Horses grazing the eastern slopes of the Bridger Mountains near Clyde Park   MSS

New colt enjoying its first spring   MSS

> *But it was the winters—when icy gales shrilled across the crusted prairies and sliced through the sturdy logs of the ranch houses, when the deadly 'white cold' crept slowly down from the Height of Land in the Canada's Northwest Territories, when snow fell interminably, burying range, stock, and ranch houses— it was the winters which finished the cattlemen.*

Joseph Kinsey Howard,
Montana: High, Wide, and Handsome

Frigid winter day near Molt MSS

Ridges of the Rocky Mountain Front piercing dense clouds LM

> **By this time of afternoon a few clouds had concocted themselves above the crest of the mountains and were drifting one after another out over the foothills below us . . . . I lost myself in watching each cloud shadow cover a hill or a portion of a ridgeline and then flow down across the coulee toward the next, as if the shadow was a slow mock flood sent by the cloud.**

Ivan Doig,
English Creek

Reynolds Peak in Glacier National Park   MSS

> *Only those able to see the pageant of evolution can be expected to value its theater, the wilderness, or its outstanding achievement, the grizzly.*

Aldo Leopold,
A Sand County Almanac

The track of the grizzly   MSS

Adult grizzly with distinctive hump   MSS

Grizzly cub getting a better look MSS

On the Big Blackfoot River above the mouth of Belmont Creek the banks are fringed by large Ponderosa pines. In the slanting sun of late afternoon the shadows of great branches reached from across the river, and the trees took the river in their arms. ""

Norman F. Maclean,
A River Runs through It

58

Blackfoot River below Clearwater Junction MSS

Arrastra Creek, a tributary to the Blackfoot River MSS

Sunset along the Yellowstone River MSS

Ice-choked Cinnabar Creek MSS

Wolverine Peak in the Beartooth Mountains   MSS

"*If you had climbed the hill behind Virginia City in 1864 and looked down the gulch you would have seen a chaotic sight. Six thousand people, almost all young men, were digging, pushing, sluicing, cursing, and fighting. Teams and heavy wagons jammed the gulch bottom, and the road, if such it could be called, was hub deep in mud from rain and obscured by dust when the road dried. Its ruts and furrows were knee deep.*

"Up to your right you could see the plumes of steam and smoke from a sawmill, turning out green boards as fast as the crew could feed logs into the whirling, belt-driven saws.

"Teams hauling logs, buildings going up, tents everywhere. And the noise, the noise of 6,000 men all in a hurry; a hurry to dig, to build, to haul, to fight, to drink— and all in hurry to get rich—and fast."

William E. Farr and K. Ross Toole,
Montana: Images of the Past

Alder Gulch near Virginia City   MSS

Grasshopper Creek near Bannack   MSS

The old and the new at Virginia City MSS

Yellowstone River near Emigrant   MSS

THE YELLOWSTONE

Millions of buffalo curried her flanks
as she shed Winter's ice in the Spring.
In the smoke of ten thousand campfires
she heard drum beats and war dances ring.
On the crest of her bosom she sped Captain Clark,
and Sacajawea as well.
She bisected prairie, the plains and the mountains
from her birth place in "John Colter's Hell."
To the trav'ler she whispered, "Come follow me,"
with a wink and a toss of her head.
She tempted the trapper, gold miner and gambler
to lie down by her sinuous bed.
"Safe passage," she murmured provocatively,
"Safe passage and riches as well."
She smiled as the thread of Custer's blue line
followed her trails and then fell.
She curved out the grade for the railroads.
She took settlers to their new home;
Watered their stock, watered their fields,
and let them grow crops on her loam.
Her banks were the goal of the trailherds.
Her grass was the prize that they sought.
'Till the blizzards of '86 and 7
nearly killed off the whole lot.
"Don't boss her, don't cross her." Let her run free,
and damn you don't dam her at all.
She's a wild old girl, let her looks not deceive you . . .
But we love her in spite of it all.

Wallace D. McRae

Custer Battlefield   MSS

December ice flows on the Yellowstone near Pompeys Pillar   MSS

The Hellroaring Plateau in the Beartooth Mountains MSS

"From the top of Montana, the wilderness seems boundless. Mountains stretch out in every direction, their peaks of jumbled granite cutting the horizon into a sawtoothed pattern of rock and snow. Flowing from the mountainsides are long plateaus, tundra-covered tables that run for miles before breaking into fields of boulders that spill steeply into distant valleys. . . . Yet the Absaroka-Beartooth has a beauty that is as subtle as tiny phlox blossoms clinging to a rocky ledge and as spectacular as a waterfall crashing hundreds of feet into a crystalline lake."

Steve Woodruff and Don Schwennesen,
Montana Wilderness

Phlox and forget-me-nots   MSS

Granite Peak, Montana's highest   MSS

Yucca at sunrise   LM

Two trumpeter swans lifting off   MSS

Nesting trumpeter   MSS

> **"** *Upper Red Rock Lake comes alive as the first golden streaks of dawn ease over the Continental Divide. A lesser scaup noisily announces the morning, accompanied by mallards quacking along the shore. . . . From one of the lake's secluded bays, two trumpeter swans add their deep, resonant bugling to the growing cacophony.* **"**

Steve Woodruff and Don Schwennesen,
Montana Wilderness

Cutoff Mountain in the Beartooth Mountains MSS

" *Snow comes early in the mountains and stays late. . . . I like snow, and I enjoy it.*

"But sometimes I find I've enjoyed about all of it I can stand. "

Stan Lynde,
Grass Roots

Snow clinging to the Anaconda-Pintler Wilderness well into June MSS

Buttercup emerging through the fading snowpack MSS

Ptarmigan with winter plumage MSS

" *Eventually, all things merge into one, and a river runs through it. The river was cut by the world's great flood and runs over rocks from the basement of time. On some of the rocks are timeless raindrops. Under the rocks are the words, and some of the words are theirs. "I am haunted by waters. "*

Norman F. Maclean,
A River Runs through It

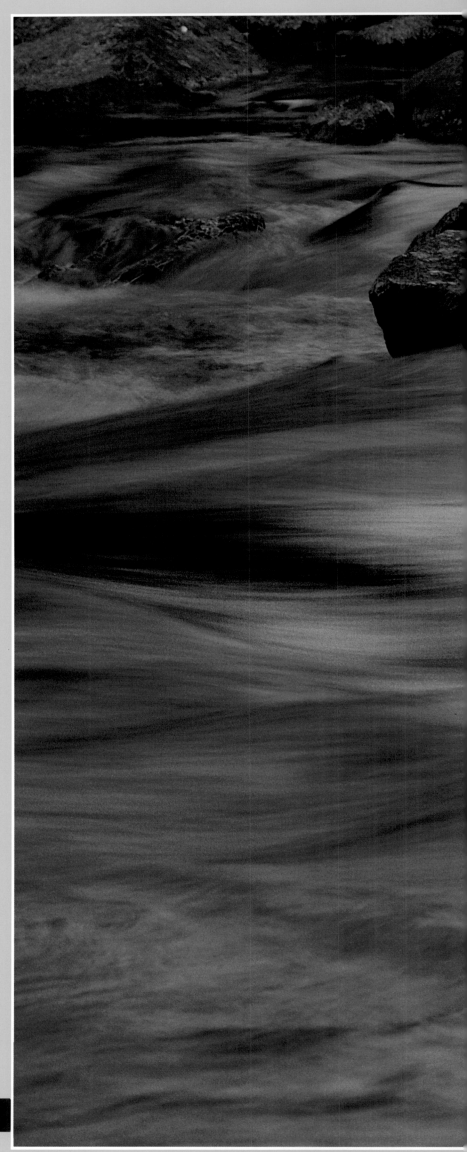

MSS

Kootenai River near Libby   MSS

Big Hole River near Divide   MSS

Yellowstone River in the Paradise Valley south of Livingston   MSS

Swan River MSS

Boulder River MSS

Smith River MSS

Stillwater River MSS

The confluence of the
Wise and Big Hole rivers MSS

Musselshell River MSS

Cottonwoods catching the last light along the Bighorn River   MSS

Along the Stillwater River   MSS

Haunting ice-forms along the West Rosebud River   MSS

Elk on the National Bison Range with the Mission Mountains as a backdrop   MSS

> **"** *The bold peaks of the Mission Mountains crown a wilderness range unique in the West both in majesty and management. Soaring more than a mile above the farms and villages of the Mission Valley, the austere western front of the Missions forms one of the most striking mountain valleys in the Rockies.* **"**

Steve Woodruff and Don Schwennesen,
Montana Wilderness

McDonald Peak, the dominant peak in the Mission Mountains   MSS

Bighorn ewe feeding   MSS

Rocky Mountain Front and Bob Marshall Wilderness west of Great Falls   LM

" *The Rocky Mountain Front, where the mountains seem to grow right out of the broad face of the prairie, conjures up images of heavy-horned sheep and broad-antlered mule deer driven to the mountain's edge by the first snows of winter.* "

Mark Henckel,
Hunter's Guide to Montana

Two large mule deer bucks MSS

Bighorn ram MSS

The Beartooth Plateau   MSS

First Lady Jean Schwinden on the farm near Wolf Point   LM

Bob Scriver and his centennial sculpture   LM

Painting churches in Baker   LM

" *If Montana is different from any other state, it is because its people like to think for themselves.* **"**

Jeannette Rankin,
in a 1972 speech

Hang glider in the Paradise Valley south of Livingston   LM

Away from it all   MSS

Handcrafting canoes in Swan Lake   LM

Float fishing the mighty
Yellowstone near Pray MSS

Ray Hurley fishing the Yellowstone
at the site of proposed Allenspur Dam MSS

Wilderness trout fishing in Upper
Quartz Lake in Glacier National Park MSS

TESTAMENT OF A FISHERMAN

*I fish because I love to; because I love the environs where trout
are found, which are invariably beautiful, and hate the environs
where crowds of people are found, which are invariably ugly;
because of all the television commercials, cocktail parties, and
assorted social posturing I thus escape; because, in a world where
most men seem to spend their lives doing things they hate,
my fishing is at once an endless source of delight and an act of
small rebellion; because trout do not lie or cheat and cannot
be bought or bribed or impressed by power, but respond only to
quietude and humility and endless patience; because I suspect that
men are going along this way for the last time, and I for one
don't want to waste the trip; because mercifully there are no
telephones on trout waters; because only in the woods can I find
solitude without loneliness; because bourbon out of an old tin
cup always tastes better out there; because maybe one day I will
catch a mermaid; and, finally, not because I regard fishing as
being so terribly important but because I suspect that so many of
the other concerns of men are equally unimportant—and
not nearly so much fun.*

Robert Traver,
Anatomy of a Fisherman

Ling fisherman on Lower Yellowstone near Huntley Irrigation Project   LM

Young angler at Lake Elmo near Billings LM

Cutthroat trout rising for a salmon fly MSS

> **"** *The sheepmen had discovered that if Montana was not exactly 'a land of milk and honey' it was a mighty good grass land and several large bands of sheep were brought on the range.* **"**

Granville Stuart,
Pioneering in Montana

Sheep along Boulder River   MSS

Sheepherder in Badger Creek northwest of Choteau   LM

Sheepherder's wagon   MSS

Smelter workers holding 100-pound dore—gold and silver—bars at a mine between Zortman and Landusky in the Little Rocky Mountains LM

Crow Fair, Crow Agency   LM

Abandoned and forgotten   MSS

> **"** *Montanans drove, tumbled and stumbled into the 20th century. The state has picked itself up and started over again many times. Its history is of a people drawn from many sources, headed toward the glowing promise of the Western frontier. It is of a people who have known the collapse of hope and the renewal of hope. It is of a people who have lived in intimacy with fear as well as courage and with cruelty as well as compassion. It is of a people who have known not only the favor but the fury of a bountiful and brooding Nature. The history of Montana is the song of a people who, repeatedly shattered, have held together, persevered and, at last, taken enduring root.* **"**

Mike Mansfield,
University of Montana Foundation

Billings ironworker   LM

Sugar beet processing plant in Sidney LM

Post mill worker on the
Flathead Indian Reservation LM

Shoveling out in Red Lodge LM

Building fence
on a ranch near Great Falls LM

" Hard work built Montana. The land gave nothing freely. Trapping, mining, cutting timber, shoveling coal, running machines, doing laundry, baking, pouring molten metal—hard work built Montana. "

William Lang and Rex Myers,
Montana: Our Land and People

Construction workers at Western Sugar Company in Billings   LM

Working hard in Montana   LM

Balsamroot starting the comeback   LM

Forest fire crowning out in the Bull Mountains   LM

Horse logging near Ronan LM

“ *Man has been cutting down trees
since he first developed tools suitable for
the job. . . . though today we realize that
what we call 'the forest products industry'
is vital to Montana's economy, few of us
realize that lumbering has been a 'root
industry' for more than a century. Had
Montana not been endowed with some
22,354,000 acres of forested land, there
could have been, for instance, very little
mining. It is difficult to see how the
railroads could have been built through the
Rockies; it is equally difficult to envision
how farmers and ranchers could have
functioned efficiently without poles, posts,
and ties.* ”

William E. Farr and K. Ross Toole,
Montana: Images of the Past

A moment of rest LM

Happy to be in Montana   MSS

“   *Because Montanans are so few and the land is so large (each person having about one-quarter of a square mile to himself on the average), the Montanan is unusually mobile, unusually informed about what his neighbors are doing, and, in spite of close personal relationships, uncommonly tolerant.*

"Strangely enough, Montanans have a strong sense of belonging—a sense which grows, perhaps, out of their common necessities. They live, after all, in a place where nature can turn a face of cold inhospitality upon them in an hour's time. Without kindness, friendship, and co-operation they could not stand up in the face of it.

"And perhaps Montanans feel that they belong, too, because of the kindredship of the old and the new. All around them are the old sights, old sounds, and old smells of the land itself. ”

K. Ross Toole,
Montana: An Uncommon Land

Airmail pilot landing in Helena LM

Jamming at the Hell Creek Bar in Jordan LM

Symbol of Montana, a cowboy in the
Bull Mountains near Musselshell LM

I am in love with Montana. For other states I have admiration, respect, recognition, even some affection, but with Montana it is love, and it's difficult to analyze love when you're in it. . . . It seemed to me that the frantic bustle of America was not in Montana. . . . The calm of the mountains and the rolling grasslands had got into the inhabitants. . . . Again my attitude may be informed by love, but it seemed to me that the towns were places to live in rather than nervous hives. People had time to pause in their occupations to undertake the passing art of neighborliness.

John Steinbeck,
Travels with Charley

Keeping the big wheels rolling
at the Montana Resources mine in Butte   LM

Lightning strike near Billings   LM

Outfitters and backpackers taking a break in the Hilgard Basin in the Madison Range   MSS

Start of the Peaks-to-Prairie relay race from Red Lodge to Billings   LM

Skipping rocks in Saint Mary Lake, Glacier National Park   MSS

Harvesting barley near Emigrant   LM

> *Modern transition notwithstanding, something remains in the state that is durably unique and uniquely durable. It is to be found in the character of the people. Montanans are formed by the vastness of a state whose mountains rise to 12,000 feet in granite massives, piled one upon another as though by some giant hand.*

Mike Mansfield,
University of Montana Foundation

Rounding up the herd   LM

Pheasant hunting in the Yellowstone Valley   MSS

Fishing Bynum Reservoir   MSS

Cheering at the Bobcats–Grizzly game at Montana State University, Bozeman LM

Successful hunt LM

Fishing, no age limitations LM

Rafting Yankee Jim Canyon on the Yellowstone River LM

Fishing the North Fork of the Blackfoot River   MSS

Canoeing the Smith River   MSS

Cow elk and newborn MSS

> " ...the camp you live in now can bost of man made things but
> your old hom is still the real out doors and when it coms to making the
> beautiful ma nature has man beat all ways from the ace and that old lady
> still owns a lot of montana... "
>
> Charles M. Russell,
> Good Medicine

Iceberg Lake in Glacier National Park MSS

Nature's designs in ponderosa pine bark   MSS

Moonrise over Crown Butte near Augusta   MSS

Mule deer does at sunrise   MSS

Eastern Montana pronghorns   MSS

Broken prairie around the Madison Buffalo Jump near Manhattan MSS

Along the Stillwater River MSS

Heaven's Peak in Glacier National Park   MSS

Along the West Rosebud River MSS

Tiger lily MSS

> **"** *To me Montana is a symphony . . . a symphony of color, painted by a thousand different plants and shrubs which set the hills ablaze— each with its own kind of inner fire.* **"**

Mike Mansfield,
University of Montana Foundation

Bitterroot, the state flower   MSS

Alpine wildflower carpet   MSS

> *Boone lay on his back and looked at a night sky shot with stars. They were sharp and bright as fresh-struck flames, like campfires that a traveler might sight on a far shore. Starlight was nearly as good as moonlight here on the upper river where blue days faded off into nights deeper than a man could believe. By day Boone could get himself on a hill and see forever, until the sky came down and shut off his eye. There was the sky above, blue as paint, and the brown earth rolling underneath, and himself between them with a free, wild feeling in his chest, as if they were the ceiling and floor of a home that was all his own.* "

A.B. Guthrie, Jr.,
The Big Sky

A.B. Guthrie, Jr., with a view
of the Rocky Mountain Front LM

The big sky, south of Browning MSS

Star tracks   MSS

Skiers on Lulu Pass near Cooke City   MSS

In the Big Belts south of Great Falls   MSS

Below Mount Clements in Glacier National Park   MSS

In the Pryor Mountains south of Billings   MSS

the photographers

MICHAEL S. SAMPLE

LARRY MAYER

Michael S. Sample began work as a professional outdoor photographer in 1970 after college and military training. In 1972 he photographed and published *Mike Mansfield's Montana,* and the following year began publishing the *Montana Calendar.* His photos have appeared in *National Geographic, Outdoor Life, Sports Afield, Time, Sierra,* and *Montana* magazines. In addition to his role as publisher of Falcon Press, which he and Bill Schneider founded in 1979, Sample spends a considerable amount of time photographing Montana. A resident of Billings since the age of six, he lives there with his wife, Barbara, and their four children.

Larry Mayer, chief photographer for the *Billings Gazette,* began his career in photojournalism in 1975 with the *Livingston Enterprise* and the *Miles City Star.* His work has been published by the *New York Times, Newsweek, U.S. News and World Report, American West,* Associated Press, United Press International, and *National Wildlife.* Born in Livingston, he now lives in Billings with his wife, Joyce, and their son, Eric.